Little River

Books by Linda McCarriston

Talking Soft Dutch
Eva-Mary
Little River

Little River

New and Selected Poems

Linda McCarriston

TriQuarterly Books
Northwestern University Press
Evanston, Illinois

TriQuarterly Books
Northwestern University Press
Evanston, Illinois 60208-4210

Printed in the United States of America

10 9 8 7 6 5 4 3 2 1

ISBN 0-8101-5132-4 (cloth)
ISBN 0-8101-5133-2 (paper)

**Library of Congress
Cataloging-in-Publication Data**
McCarriston, Linda.
    Little river : new and selected poems /
Linda McCarriston.
        p. cm.
    ISBN 0-8101-5132-4 (cloth : alk. paper) —
    ISBN 0-8101-5133-2 (pbk. : alk. paper)
    I. Title

PS3563.C3357 L58 2002
813'.54—dc21

                                    2001054430

The paper used in this publication meets
the minimum requirements of the American
National Standard for Information Sciences—
Permanence of Paper for Printed
Library Materials, ANSI Z39.48-1984.

There's no use to taking the Devil
to law if the court is held in Hell.

Irish saying

Contents

Acknowledgments	ix
Kitchen Terrarium: 1983	3
In Off the Cliffs of Moher	9
Stone Quarry: Late Capitalism Comes to the Remote West Coast of Ireland	10
Knockeven	11
Local	12
In Clare	13
Aubade	14
As Memory	16
At the Indian Store	19
Reading *Ode to the West Wind* 25 Years Later	21
At My House	23
Postcard: Louise to Thelma, from Hippy Writing School	25
The Greeks	26
Harvard Housing	27
Indian Country	29
Exxon	29
Piggly Wiggly	30
Last Frontier	32
Ashtray: A Study	34
Alder Drive: Anchorage	35
In Mr. Rogers' Neighbourhood	36
January, Anchorage	37
With the Horse in the Winter Pasture	41
Bucked	42

Quincey's Harvest Moon   43

On Horseback   44

"Girl from Lynn Bathes Horse!"   46

Riding Out at Evening   48

Riding Moriah in October   50

Le Coursier de Jeanne D'Arc   52

Aubade: November   55

A Thousand Genuflections   56

Green   59

Frontier   61

Traditional   63

Two Stories for Angel on the
    1st Anniversary of Her Sobriety   64

Wrought Figure   66

Warrior   68

The Devil   69

Blow-Up   70

Mercato   72

Elm Street: October 1977   73

Face   74

Medicine for the Woman Betrayed   75

Anniversary   76

Swan Lake: Kenai Wilderness, Alaska   77

Song of the Scullery   79

Katherine   80

"My Fellow Americans . . ."   82

Letter to the Daughter-in-Heart   84

Workshop   86

Transit   87

Little River   89

Spring at the Bunting Institute, 1993   91

Acknowledgments

For the many kinds of help and encouragement I have received over the period during which these poems were written, I must thank the Mary Ingraham Bunting Institute of Radcliffe College, the Jenny McKean Moore Foundation at George Washington University, and the University of Alaska Anchorage: my colleagues, my students, my friends.

Thanks to the following magazines in which these poems appeared:

The Atlantic: "Wrought Figure"

Cedar Hill: "Alder Drive: Anchorage," "Face," "Frontier"

Electric Acorn: "'Girl from Lynn Bathes Horse!'"

George Washington Review: "The Devil," "Green," "Traditional," "Two Stories for Angel on the 1st Anniversary of Her Sobriety"

Georgia Review: "*Le Coursier de Jeanne D'Arc*"

Green Mountains Review: "Little River," "Song of the Scullery"

Heart: "Letter to the Daughter-in-Heart," "Workshop"

Kalliope: "Blow-Up"

Luna: "'My Fellow Americans . . . ,'" "Warrior"

Ohio Review: "With the Horse in the Winter Pasture"

Plum Review: "Anniversary," "*In Mr. Rogers' Neighbourhood*"

Poetry: "Bucked," "On Horseback," "Quincey's Harvest Moon," "Riding Out at Evening"

Poetry Flash: "Swan Lake"

Poetry Northwest: "Reading *Ode to the West Wind* 25 Years Later"

Prairie Schooner: "Last Frontier," "*Mercato*"

Sojourner: "Kitchen Terrarium: 1983"

Sojourners: "At the Indian Store"

Stinging Fly (Ireland): "Stone Quarry: Late Capitalism Comes to the Remote West Coast of Ireland," "Swan Lake"

Tar River Poetry: "Stone Quarry: Late Capitalism Comes to the Remote West Coast of Ireland"

TriQuarterly: "Elm Street: October 1977," "The Greeks," "A Thousand Genuflections"

Little River

Kitchen Terrarium: 1983

No, not much, the old song
travels back to me from memory,
from when I was your age.
I don't want my arms around you,
I don't bless the day I found you,
no, not much. Old standards,
tender and sad, surprise me,
reminding me of you, the child
I miss more than ever I missed
a lover. Everywhere are brown-
haired boys in jeans. Everywhere
are mothers who barely notice
as the school bus stops, starts up
with its long sigh, and the kids
bang in, their voices still running
at bus-din pitch, the dog leaping
hip-high beside them, to hit
the first flat surface with a stew
of papers and books. You aren't
here, upending my kitchen, hungry
and loud. You won't go off to play
these narrowing afternoons at dusk
as you have all the Octobers,
each of which, like single afternoons
heading toward this one, has borne
more dark than the last, its thin light
bullied down to this darkest October.
Soon we'll set the clocks back.
I dread it – the black outside the windows,

each window a mirror reflecting
empty space, your face not there,
intent over paper, your body
not boogeying by, preoccupied, nothing
of you here, not even your place
when I turn to set plates on the table.

II

All day in front of the judge
and before we began I knew the outcome.
I wore a dress. I presented myself as
a lady – the least and easiest
of selves, but there the best that is said
of a woman, and the face that requires
no reprisal. Your father the doctor,
vested in white, had come to say
he was ready. And with him the lawyer,
making truth out of lies and money.
All day the expert testimony fell
– words of strangers, words from books
written by governors for the sake
of governors – on the city that was
childhood: your life with me, its thousand
streets, each with its hundred
houses, each of these with its many rooms,
its multifold ordered contents built up
by love's long attentions over years.

When the judge rose, in the gown
of a woman, to speak his decision, I rose
– straining in my blood's roar to hear him.

The part he read straight at me
was where he called you a man: by dictum
the great excision had begun, the boy
from the woman. In my mind's eye
I saw you outside the courthouse
partway up a tree, where you'd climbed
to see if parallel streets could meet
on some far horizon: a sixth grade boy,
four foot nine, who still gave
turns to the teddies he slept with.
It might have been the Judgment of Solomon,
but the judge was not wise. He halved
the child, and the false mother gloated
– thumbs up – at the glad decree.
Had I hoped something different would happen
there, blind stone the only woman in the
chamber besides me? Did I think he would
want you whole, this judge, halved,
like the rest – he cannot remember it –
and hardened into a man?

III

Today at the kitchen table I write
the one letter your father lets by

each week. Then I write postcards
I can't send yet. I'm ahead of myself,
a backlog of longing for even

the least hello: *Are you ready
for skiing?*, I enthuse on the back
of the photo – a swirl of white

at the knees of the red-suited
athlete – as if it were you
in the picture, as if I, not there

on the slope beside you, were just
out of sight, cheering, making

the paper memory. In fact, it's still
only October. You're still only

a boy, and your father is by you now,
instructing. He takes you to town.
You get new skis. The season ticket,

the flashy gear. He takes you for walks
and shows you the husk of, say, milkweed,
the alien, gestative thing. You go

with him to the high ground we found,
the place you people with Indians,
and he points out the elm that dominates

that splendid, open space: *a winner*,
not *a loser* around. He takes you
to dine.

But when you phone me

your voice is hollow for what lives here
in this house of less: *There's nobody home,*
just the housekeeper. There's everything
here, but it's empty. There isn't

a kitchen. Axis Mundi of the Lesser World,
I sit in it as you left it, the heat
from the cookstove, the grain of the
table under my hand less palpable

to my own flesh than the sadness
in you which fades against his gifts, his novitiate's
walks, but booms up, sudden, around you

like someone's old favourite turned loud
on the radio. Davey, if we are to sing
of each other in common terms, we must
use words long worn sore with meaning:

the rare soft moments of a hard lust, satisfied,
held up as love's highest figure. It is this
instruction into which you've been taken

to grow, like the moss and lichen
still alive here, that you gathered
and placed in the big glass jar on the table.
The glass is clear. From inside it must be

invisible, so there would be an Emperor
of the Jar and for his son
a place beside him, to which all of creation

had been scaled: no trees taller than
a man to climb, no creatures
but pets and game, a mirror to look at
and walk upon, that he would tell you is *water.*

In Off the Cliffs of Moher

This is the wind they say makes people
mad here. Bare-legged after her bath
she is lying on the sofa by the window

as if watching a flock of birds at a feeder –
colour, ardor, flight. I have not been here
long enough to guess what such a wind

might do, season after season, to a woman,
to a man. But the sheep, I can see, all day
mill up and back among the tatters of the

stone pasture fences: restlessness, neglect
in the dooryards of before, and the grazing
ghosts the wind won't let leave home.

Stone Quarry: Late Capitalism Comes
to the Remote West Coast of Ireland

From here stones were drawn
for the ruin in the distance,
stones for walls fallen
and falling, for cottages

empty and roofless
along this road,
for fences holding

the gate to the lane.
Cattle and sheep graze
its brink as they grazed

the centuries gutted.
But now comes by night
– who used to steal slate –

the man in new guise.
Dead cars and garbage
– what costs to dispose of –

are what he brings back here,
signs of abundance,
the colourful tumble of

rubbish down scree of
black-gray. Will earth here
as sea has, as history

has, develop a taste
for, develop a stomach
to take it and eat it
digesting even its name?

Knockeven

for Jessie

Black stones weaving
up the weaving grass
like sheep, and sheep grazing
the green depths like
stones. The wind is working

all of it all day, a pumice,
roughly. The waters though

find their own way deep
in the runnels that their toil
has made going about going
elsewhere gravely
though their music is gay.

Local

In an Irish pub, vatican
of stout and *fags*, I travel back
a family generation, to the land
of *an honest man's failing.* With such

no other island is so richly
endowed. I myself was many years
inclined to honesty but now deceive
myself perhaps and others, having come

a decade – more – ago to the crossroad
where the pure refusal of a drunk's
grave meets the compromise of walking
the crooked lane conscious.

I cannot bear to watch the man
who so delights them in a parody
of dance but watch them watch him
with smiles that shine communal and

benign, whose brother, just months past,
himself was swept – like an ill-advised
explorer in the ocean-caves below
this Fisher Street bar – away

in the gay and honest waves of drink
turned savage in the innerworld, turned
toothed and clawed in the changeless
village tide that always turns.

In Clare

Michael was who she loved and was not loved by
though she was lovely as a silken thing, blue-eyed and good.
In the stern of the mail-boat with loaves of store-bought bread
she sat, and the wind wrapped her face in her yellow hair.
Every door to her soul was open. The boat carried her
out from him and away. Ahead lay the island in rain. Her eyes
travelled inward deep as outward opened the bay.

Aubade

for W.D.

After the night of music
– small smoky pubs and every fiddle
played by a friend – after you'd walked
to a bed the one with trouble
walking, and driven another back home,
buying pints (the county *Da*) for a few
in between – we rode the yarrow-
lighted lanes back to the silent farm,
goats waiting in the yard for the car
to sleep on, two long-legged kids and
a leaping nanny *good luck for a farm*,

and dogs, the cows asleep for the night,
the ponies likewise out on the deep-scored
high midsummer green,
wind and yellow light, the days-long
burnishing day shining each
brief life immaculate,

we sat at the kitchen table,
ate bread with jam,
drank a cup of tea, cleaned up and
went to your bed
for the few hours until the cows would call you
to the tune of goat hooves
playing the roof of the car. The stars
were ours, then hand in hand, bow
to curve, we dozed
as the dark withdrew

and gave slow light to the swallows,
to the words we'd given
each other, which were few and kind and true.
Carried into keeping were
our bodies, close as two worn meadows
along a historied wall.

As Memory

I believe I will not be blown away
tonight from the corner of this fine
high house in Ireland. I believe the rain
– nightmare hands of it long-fingered
grasping from the roofline – will not
pinch the latched window open, not
push the door to. I am not the mare
buffeted, days now, in the pasture
below me, head down, rump to the sea,
worn so out from standing she won't
graze. *Child at the window*, a voice
says, *Heart, come to the table for tea.*

At the Indian Store

I could not presume even to speak of it
were we to meet, were we to be trapped
together in a storm, on a bus, say,
even sharing the least meal there.
Watching you from across the store,
I hardly dare let you catch me –
full-blooded Comanche, your skin the colour
human, your face magnificent, intent,
a flint in a time and town as sodden
and rich as a pudding. Was ever so much
taken from so many? Was ever
so little learned? The city's thin
veneer of glass and concrete is streets
a generation deep, and everything
the colour white, the colour paper money.
And I am here putting my feet down
on what I do not know. And over my head
I do not know. I am buying turquoise
and silver, beads, a recording of what
a few remember and sing from the beds
of pickup trucks, from a time
when a people knew on what they stood
and under. I was a sportsman
on the shooting trains that slaughtered
herds of buffalo so great they spread,
before I came, to the plains horizon.
I was the hand of the government
that gave you, with the word for gift,
blankets of smallpox to cover you
the apocalyptic winters. I broke

the promises that were not made
of frivolous things but of the great things.
Yet I am woman and know the hunger
of homelessness, the abyss of the great lie,
the gifts of sickness and injury. My whiteness
is a man in me, and I am likewise his stranger.
From me as well goes handiwork, for pennies,
out to the streets of Tulsa this dusk
on the dead-white flesh of the fathers.

Reading *Ode to the West Wind* 25 Years Later

The class was large. All girls.
The nun was old. And never was one.
I don't recall we ever read
a fiery word, but took
her dictation – *understanding* –
hunk by hunk down in the margins:

this *meant* this and that *meant*
that. We toiled like mites
mining the floor of the too-high
room, the tall air above us
thick with invisible stacks of the
critical argument – eternal,

indivisible – vowel by consonant
descending. Here and there
something in a
footnote
up there would rile her,
as though she observed

the secret squabbles of angels.
Forgive me, Sister
WhoeverYouWere, in your costume, built,
it seemed, from the stove-pipe
section of the hardware, but black
was your *metier*, and white; the poem was

text, windless, tone-deaf, and unsexed.
It *meant* and it *meant* literary
referent, and the pale wad
of your face under the wimple
refused it even distant, scintillant music
of the spheres. Dust and stillness,

scribbling meaningless
things into the print, I bent with
the others, as if over a poisoned
apple, as Step-mother, agent of
literary darkness, breathed wrought
burnished metal into rust.

At My House

My mother's resumé at seventy-eight –
    who has worked as many years
        as she's smoked cigarettes,
since she was fourteen buying Cubebs,
    eight cents a pack, cleaning houses;
        buying Wings at thirteen cents
with her first real job – Corns. Bunions.
    Varicose veins. *By the time I could afford*
        good shoes I didn't need them,
after the Old Man died. Luncheonette,
    box factory, a decade in the meat room.
    Home. Into her seventies,
Star Market's "Dorothy Muriel," flats
    of rolls and sweetbreads to wrangle.
    Retired for the fourth time
she was seventy-four. *I had a real bad pair once*
    waitressing. That's the ugly bunion,
    – she touches it, sitting on the porch stoop
smoking, my nearby garden a figment
    to her and distant – *they can take those*
        off now. I can still feel how those
damn shoes killed me. Where the grass
    drops through brush to a little river
        the dog and cat curl in shade,
the words of the stream purl around us. *Sometimes*
    no one could see I'd take the damn things off
    and work back there in my stockings.

Now she says *Sit*, meaning
    take here with me what was
        a lifetime withheld. Get off
your feet, drain the chronic ache
    from your legs, drop your cheap shoes
        to the side, let your ankles
unswell. I cannot fathom
    how radical it is for her to do
        nothing: Not To
garden not to walk read write not
    stand and put lipstick on
        in the mirror, as though
it were under a boss's nose: *I won't.*
    I'm punched out for good.
        Where is the pleasure in it?

What is/was pleasure? The other
    side, any year, of where
        she was standing? Something
You buy? This is the seat
    she paid for with her life, and if
        she dreamed a different destination
ever, she isn't fool enough
    to know so now. Sometimes
        I hear coming from her, where
she's pitted against the summons to rise,
    a roar like the hollow
        almost-silence of a canyon.

Postcard: Louise to Thelma, from Hippy Writing School

– Tail End of the Sixties –

Nobody here gets clap
or heartbreak. Even
Legionnaire's Disease
couldn't march in
so little is contagious –

mono, maybe, for the sake
of its name and what
one might make of it. All
the real diseases people
give each other stop

at the bump in the road
– mumps or measles –
even a greasy hepatitis
only gets in on a needle,
something done solo,

like love.

The Greeks

Washington, D.C.

"Brothers," they live in houses unfettered
by mothers, by sisters, by the battle
of the sexes or by any other
at odds. Neighbours they are to me here
and I watch them, drawn to the window by their night-
cries in the street: glass
breaking, fist-fighting, heart-breaking, poison
fun. They intrigue me these sons of moneyed fathers,
monotheists, white boys next day sobering
up on patches of dirt packed outside
where they dwell: castles like crack houses,
rags draping windows, the strange facelessness
that filth gives to a gilded building.
On scavenged lawn chairs in daylight
they recline, in what way not the panhandlers
on the heat vent one block down I cannot
say, but power has passed down many hands
to reach them here rehearsing for
the world their fathers made them, silver
spoon and silver tray. Good brown
whores visit of an evening, and daughters
of their own fathers dress high to call, bewitched
as well by the lustre of the old order.
Even on this block it is clear
what this gestation is meant to prepare them
to preside over is gone. They could as well be
whooping in face-paint and feathers, facing
their fathers' fathers' fathers, as be
reeling on the street at 3 A.M. deaf
to the polyphonic silence that surrounds them.

Harvard Housing
for RDG

The old neighbourhood is gone. Taupe
and khaki clapboards trim the new
buildings, architected to befriend what is left
of the Irish: doorways lacquered loudly
red or purple, curtained with lace, the scale
small and particular, vestiges of garden
gate and fence against the cluster-housing
where nothing but shapes congregate.

The tasteful-unto-invisibility structures
empty, by day, the pathways empty that
once couched stoop-sitters, fence-
talkers baby-walkers, children let out
to play, somewhat safely, mixed breed dogs
and cats that bred loosely and whelped
in closets, in brambly underporches
shadowed by lathe. Nights are quiet.
No fights? No love-making? No: no
windows open: central heat, central air.
No coal. No mosquitoes. (No chickens.)

In suits and bearing slim leather cases
in which lie side by side paper sheets
of words and figures that are their mops
and wrenches, the nouveau R.C. Kelly
Streeters beep their Saabs un-
locked mornings and slip fitly in,
good teeth braced perfect and preserved
in gold, long legs tight knees and
asses. Woolmark, the label. Precision cuts.

Then come the groundskeepers in to lay
mulch, to manure the rose bushes. Tim
and James. The rubbishmen, street-
sweepers, Donal, Pat, hollering. Then
come the women singly, not calling
to one another, in cheap sneakers
and polyester pull-ons, with keys,
letting themselves in to clean
in potatoey legs and t-shirts stamped
with local joints' logos. At Sage's
a freckled blue-eyed redhead maybe forty
rings the cash register, nights, after
a long office day, making the mortgage.
The corner crossing guard's gone home
– to kids or to a second job – who,
hand raised against traffic and Claddagh ring
shining like her must-be-second-generation-Irish
-cop's mug, daily crosses me over
at Concord and Huron, crosses me back.

Indian Country

The land was ours before we were the land's ...
Robert Frost

Your face is the face of my family enemy ...
Lucille Clifton

Exxon

At the gas station on Apache land, my fair-
haired friend, my hale-fellow-well-met
businessman friend, my moon-faced, moon-
shadowless silky blond-whisped and blue blue
eyed friend, determined hand-pumper, insists
he will pump the hand of the attendant who
has pumped our gas. The station stands –
given how we think of things – at the heart
of a desolation of land so vast it flattens my
eastern imagination. Under its gray
flow the absence of water, the absence of
mineral wealth. Poverty of Ariel. Poverty of Caliban
as well. Done, paid, Apache wheels back
into his station – small and glass, a case in the Fogg Museum
in which he might stand as a rare stone,
brilliant and pitiless, shimmering rage.
The black of his hair is strength
enough, but a light fires
his skin, his eyes, as if a cable
underfoot – a robbery alert,
a warning buzzer – sent a million volts
into his spine from below the poured concrete
of the island. Moon-face WILL: *I never did anything
to him*, as he hops from the mini pickup...

Get in.
Shut up. They will never find us out here
or the little truck or your fucking stupid grin.
Get in, O Heartless History-
less Creeper of Surfaces, heir, ignorant grandson
of Grand Forgetting, or take your broadcloth
oxford shirt off and stand before him, suck your white
gut in, and as if to enter that tiny blinding space in which
he stands as if it were sacred, raise a hand.

Piggly Wiggly

In the market I am grateful to be
small, a woman, dark-haired, straight- haired,
poor with poor prospects, grateful
for my teeth – universal calender
of the poor: the months'-long decay, candy
a nickel at a time and aspirin, the gutting of what's left
without novocain, which you couldn't afford.
Top forty, thinner even than in winter K-Marts
pitiful back east, hokier than in on hold, the phone's
hollow glad-hand – wands into the massive empty space
like gas. Women, children, silent, few
pick their way among canned flaked frozen as though
some god had boxed up grief and set it down here
– this flat-roofed cinderblock in desolation –
for the white guy to make his buck on
hot cross buns and Twinkies.

White bread, peanut butter in my basket
raisins, company store prices, no one speaking
to me or to each other, no suburban chirping

guiding wagons to their rightful places, no old-town
catcalls of the open market, no penny ante haggling.
Dead. And the thing
vacuumed from this air – the square building and the land
on which it stands – and replaced with cheese
in spray cans, food stamps and glare, seemed to be merely
wind once across empty spaces, seemed to be nothing
as it gave itself freely and freely took itself away.

Last Frontier

Divorced, fifty, she took the first
good job that offered itself,
outfitted a pickup and drove alone
to Alaska. It was not her myth.

It was a man's myth, odometer
rolling over every tenth of the 5
thousand miles, like dice.
Who knew what could happen?

How many spruces did she pass?
They turned from Norway to Red
to Sitka, the lakes went from bass-
black to the blue of glacier. Her

myth had been the pie at the end
of the rainbow she'd polished for
thirty years: mother, wife.
Her myth was just this side of

tatting doilies: clapboard house
painted white, time, finally,
to write, her kids and their kids,
yes, coming Sundays, one of the

men whose lives she'd lugged
– various and weighty as tinkers'
wagons – by her. But for the
sending switch in the oil pressure

unit, she made the trip event-
lessly, her dog (sleeping days
while she drove) at night played
the role of grown son or husband:

watched out. Her first year
done with – her 51st year – she
recalls the memorable best of it:
a manicure every second

Saturday in a cinderblock
stripmall. Stormy, her nail tech.

Ashtray: A Study

A Rorschach of tar shaped like a misshapen
heart, right atrium enlarged, itself bilobed,

piled now, though emptied after each smoke,
with neat ash-sheaves, at the centre of which,

when I flick, is a miniscule red glow, a coal
for the grate of a dollhouse. Rectangle, in fact,

it's the lid of another rectangle, deeper still,
a gift container for, no doubt, special things,

rings, a necklace. Its shape, its porcelain
designs of blue and red on white, Chinese,

repeat. I am reminded of sarcophagi in which
lie side by side Egyptian royal couples. On top:

a moulting butterfly? A hummingbird? A stem,
a blossom. No two of anything on this coffin.

Alder Drive: Anchorage

Twenty below, and no snow
to bank foundations, dark and
cold become the one thing –
mouth of the arctic night

closed on us. I draw the heavy
drapes against the sight, turn
the leaves of the hanging plants

away, count the cats and dogs, the lights
and say out loud inside my bubble
safe, the way a child might,

but my son's face rises – so
distant tonight, little boat, peril
of a young man's life –

his voice, too, outside the window.

In Mr. Rogers' Neighbourhood

The frame of every door that locks
is split. Somebody lived here to whom
privacy was forbidden. I have known many
who, their whole lives through, never
would presume to close a door
on the man who *put food on the table
for the children.* Front door, back door,
bedroom, bathroom, any safe place
off the kitchen, torn.

I have seen the rage rattle in the knob,
have heard the shoulder take on the hollow-core
as it might an intruder, have watched it
flimsy as a thin veneer that covers an idea
massive and nasty and old, buckle and give.
Told by those expert in the subject that
what I live in now is loneliness, I live
alone: in all the doorjambs here the faults
are silent, but for the sounds I hear
even when I wish not to listen. I ought not

to dwell on it, I tell myself. I smelled
bread baking when I came here with the realtor,
I saw the pink girls' bedroom and the toys,
the mama bear papa bear baby bear
coats in a row on their hangers. I ought
not to dwell alone, I tell myself as well,
wishing, still, for the lighted window,
as though I had not spent my life
studying the fire inside.

January, Anchorage

The street is a string of baby
birds, beaks open: trucks,' cars'

hoods up waiting for a jump.
Is everything made of dry ice?

Everything is steaming.
Trees so layered in rime they've lost

twig definition bloom as luminous
cones of cotton candy. Street signs:

mossed in white. "I'm lost," I call on
my cell, "at the corner of Frost

and Frost." Into week three of
25 below, no snow, the blue

daytime sky so like the sky of a
life-enhancing planet, the night-

sky knives pierce the blackblue
fabric deeper every evening.

Metal is stressed to breaking.
Clutch pedal to the floor like lifting,

from under, a snowladen bulkhead
door. Through window glass I look out.

In, I listen as the furnace turns
over turns over in my house of old

toast, the spaces around outlets
taped to blunt the scalpels of cold.

Underground, natural gas is streaming
here to warm me in hidden lines I

hardly believe in. Earthquake country.

With the Horse in the Winter Pasture

Zero degrees, no wind, and barely
the January sun has begun to ripen.
You, who all day yesterday
brooked with your body
a brutal storm from the north,
now graze as amiably over the snow
and hay as if it were August.
Or more so: free of the flies, free
of the rider – bit, crop, and fetter.
What we endure need not turn us to stone,
insists the gray bird in the birch-on-blue,
who survives in her three least notes.
And so, today, I am victim
of nothing, nor am I mistress, just
hanging around the sun-catching corner
as if it were after school, a fool,
a woman carrying on like a girl.
I throw my arm over your withers
and bury my face in your neck:
white plush, pulse, smell
of woodsmoke. The child is alive
who prayed by her bed to die.

Bucked

Balanced for that instant
in midair, I watched
his rump, in white slow-motion
rise – heart-cleft, perfect –
to deliver the awesome blow.

How beautiful the muscles
of the world in their uses!
Great limbs of trees, waves
scaling seawalls, the moon's
dreadful flex on everything,

heart valves and minute
vessels, the spiralled cues
for weakness that I pass on
to my children: of which
might one ask to be spared?

Quincey's Harvest Moon

All the day the wind has ruffled
the fading green, the way a man
might rough and tumble-up his dog,
his old dog – fondly, mock-savage.
September is like that. Goodbye
tired fields I rode through,
grumpy softwoods growing stiffer
every morning, dowagers, dear cronies.
And late tonight, feigning
domestic chores outside, I join
the gravid harvest moon barely clearing
the ridge, to visit the old horse.
In the near pasture, I say her name
– not loudly, not a call –
under the blood-and-gutsy moon that shapes
with forge-light the mountain,
the orchard, the fine back
and rump and neck of the mare.
Of course she walks toward me,
as on all the nights of all the years,
bearing her star ahead of her
on her own field of dark: the bay,
gracious gift of her body.
Square off the horizon that star comes,
will come for years, a new beast
in the sky of the heart's imagination.
We smell each other. She takes
the apple. I hold her head again, watching
even this heartiest, goldenest of moons up
and up transpire, ever paler,
more distant, to spirit.

On Horseback

for the McFauns

We are only walking.
This is not the romance
of horseback riding:
your mane, which is short
and scraggly, sticks out
like a hedge of cowlicks
or merely flops off to the side.
Nothing is flying, trans–
porting, transcendent.

Then we aren't a metaphor
for anything, Shawnee James,
little borrowed horse I learn on.
Your body is bent and dented
as the first car I owned,
the '52 Plymouth, brush-painted,
one walleye headlight
held in with masking tape.
And I am a comparable model.

But, cast off the road,
our shadow is travelling
across the cut stubble of October.
My hands have forgotten themselves,
as the shadow has forgotten them,
does not require them.
With your four legs, our two heads
find a balance.

A single thing in gray,
its many muscles flush and flexing
in everyday grace,
we move over the grass, as whole
as the shape anything makes, passing.
We are something going somewhere,
handsome and practical and proud.
We shake out our tail.

"Girl from Lynn Bathes Horse!"

1100 pounds, more or less, the mare
high-steps a trot on a short circle
– two feet of line from the hand
of the Tenement Kid who never outgrew
the wish to be able to do this
to the head of the horse who never
watched TV, never saw the Lone Ranger
or Hoppy, never read about Smoky or
Flicka, Black Beauty or King of the Wind,
and so cannot possibly know that the only
thing the two of them need to perform
this difficult, dangerous act together

is love, the kind between cowgirl and pony,
infused as the Garden's knowing. To hell
with experience, instruction, example,
coin of the grownup world. You don't
really need what you don't really own.

In her off hand the stiff hose kinks,
coiling underfoot as the mare circles,
hating the green snake, the water that spurts,
urging her faster, crosser at every turn,
in the tight well of mud, in the slick-
footing'd flood of the yard. *It's a lot like
washing a car*, she quips, as a shod hoof
flies out when the wet slaps horse privates –
It's always like something else, this life

for which squirting a half-ton of horse-in-hand
on the strength of a nine-year-old's metaphysics
is a figure for all the rest, for the morning
by morning invention of a self
in the laboratory of unmarked chemicals.

Childhood is the barrel they give you
to go over the falls in. Whatever you get to take
with you in it can't be bigger or sharper
than an idea. It must be that fall, clenched
in a kid's fist (as earth expresses a diamond),
that transforms it from simply Some Dumb Thing
to Some Dumb Thing that is magic,
the fifth essence, perhaps, what the alchemists
knew lay latent in every thing. Even the least.
Even the most ridiculous.

Riding Out at Evening

At dusk, everything blurs and softens.
From here out over the long valley,
the fields and hills pull up
the first slight sheets of evening,
as, over the next hour,
heavier, darker ones will follow.

Quieted roads, predictable deer
browsing in a neighbour's field, another's
herd of heifers, the kitchen lights
starting in many windows. On horseback
I take it in, neither visitor
nor intruder, but kin passing, closer
and closer to night, its cold streams
rising in the sugarbush and hollow.

Half-aloud, I say to the horse,
or myself, or whoever: *let fire not come
to this house, nor that barn,
nor lightning strike the cattle.
Let dogs not gain the gravid doe, let the lights
of the rooms convey what they seem to.*

And who is to say it is useless
or foolish to ride out in the falling light
alone, wishing, or praying,
for particular good to particular beings
on one small road in a huge world?
The horse bears me along, like grace,

making me better than what I am,
and what I think or say or see
is whole in these moments, is neither
small nor broken. For up, out of
the inscrutable earth, have come my body
and the separate body of the mare:
flawed and aching and wronged. Who then
is better made to say *be well, be glad,*

or who to long that we, as one,
might course over the entire valley,
over all valleys, as a bird in great embrace
of flight, who presses against her breast,
in grief and tenderness,
the whole weeping body of the world?

Riding Moriah in October

Each leaf
has its goblin

and horses, whose
eyes are different

from ours, see
each of them

all of them –
the whole hillside

glittering –
the gold and the

crimson, magenta
which over the edge of

the knobs of the
goblin stick up

the eyes of
the goblin glare down

like Clem with his
nose hanging over.

I praise her who
trots out in wind

like this, whose
hoof on the

earth is a ten-
tative

thing, who would if I
let her – who did, I

swear, in a life
before this one –

lose filly heart,
take filly wing.

Le Coursier de Jeanne D'Arc

You know that they burned her horse
before her. Though it is not recorded,
you know that they burned her Percheron
first, before her eyes, because you

know that story, so old that story,
the routine story, carried to its
extreme, of the cruelty that can make
of what a woman hears *a silence,*

that can make of what a woman sees
a lie. She had no son for them to burn,
for them to take from her in the world
not of her making and put to its pyre,

so they layered a greater one in front of
where she was staked to her own –
as you have seen her pictured sometimes,
her eyes raised to the sky. But they were

not raised. This is yet one of their lies.
They were not closed. Though her hands
were bound behind her, and her feet were
bound deep in what would become fire,

she watched. Of greenwood stakes
head-high and thicker than a man's waist
they laced the narrow corral that would not
burn until flesh had burned, until

bone was burning, and laid it thick
with tinder – fatted wicks and sulphur,
kindling and logs – and ran a ramp
up to its height from where the gray horse

waited, his dapples making of his flesh
a living metal, layers of life
through which the light shone out
in places as it seems to through the flesh

of certain fish, a light she knew
as purest, coming, like that, from within.
Not flinching, not praying, she looked
the last time on the body she knew

better than the flesh of any man, or child,
or woman, having long since left the lap
of her mother – the chest with its
perfect plates of muscle, the neck

with its perfect, prow-like curve,
the hindquarters' – pistons – powerful cleft
pennoned with the silk of his tail.
Having ridden as they did together

– those places, that hard, that long –
their eyes found easiest that day
the way to each other, their bodies
wedded in a sacrament unmediated

by man. With fire they drove him
up the ramp and off into the pyre
and tossed the flame in with him.
This was the last chance they gave her

to recant her world, in which their power
came not from God. Unmoved, the Men
of God began watching him burn, and better,
watching her watch him burn, hearing

the long mad godlike trumpet of his terror,
his crashing in the wood, the groan
of stakes that held, the silverblack hide,
the pricked ears catching first

like driest bark, and the eyes.
And she knew, by this agony, that she
might choose to live still, if she would
but make her sign on the parchment

they would lay before her, which now
would include this new truth: that it
did not happen, this death in the circle,
the rearing, plunging, raging, the splendid

armour-coloured head raised one last time
above the flames before they took him
– like any game untended on the spit – into
their yellow-green, their blackening red.

Aubade: November

Waking, on the day of Saint Cecilia,
to the first snowfall lavish enough
to cover, I hear music, of which
she is the patroness, Handel,
making the old praise to her
that holds up still, even over
the clock radio.
        First up, I go
to feed the mare and turn her out.
In flannel gown, robe and parka,
clumsy boots that ground me
in my bulk, I let my spirit mount
as she bounds out into the snow,
shaking her head in mock menace,
giving the falling sky *what for*
with her heels.
        Say this life
that I carry is small enough. Say
I know the worlds beyond it, know
that mine can be neither earned nor fair.
Still there come to me moments of such
joy and forgiveness that I seem
to be hurting nothing, that nothing
seems to be hurting me.
        Inside,
I start the day's fire. The room
assumes patterns of warmth that swirl
as the birds do over the snowy garden.
Turbulent, tossed this way and that
like a single mind in torment,
they take brief shape over the stalks
gone to seed, and come to rest.

A Thousand Genuflections

Winter mornings when I call her,
out of falling snow she trots
into view, her tail and mane
made flame by movement, carrying,
as line and motion, back into air
her shape and substance – like fire
into heat into light, turns
the candle takes, burning.
And her head – her senses,
every one is a scout sent out
ahead of her, behind, beside:
her eye upon me, over the distance,
her ear, its million listeners,
delicate and vast her nose, her mouth,
her voice upon me, closing the distance.
I could just put the buckets down
and go, but I kneel to hold them
as she eats, as she drinks, to be
this close. For something of myself
lives here, stripped of the knowing
that is not knowing, a single thing
from the least webbed tissues
of the heart straight out to the tips
of the guardhairs that shimmer off
beyond my sight into air, the grasses,
grain, the water, light.
I've come like this each day
for years across the hard winters,
seeing a figure for the thing itself,

divine – appetite and breath,
flesh and attention. This morning
her presence asks of me: *And might
you be your body? Might we be
not the figure, but the thing itself?*

Green

Barely done with growing but enough
done for use, big and brand-new
to themselves, and to us fresh-minted,

the bodies of boys on the last laps
toward manhood, by which we mean
humanness, are harvested. Shocks

of them are bound and sent
still green, to ripen
in the shipping like tropical

produce. They have achieved
size. They have produced mass —
arms and legs, the back's long

muscles, unlined quick strong hands.
It is as though we do not know
that they are boys still, that

they have souls, still boys', to which
the dander of the world clings,
benign or malignant, irritant

or balm to the willow-green nap
of the soul. Barely have they
stopped being measured against

the doorframe, bringing the pencil
and tape to another and pressing
hard against the jamb up toward

adulthood. It is as though we do not
know they are our sons, and do not
know they are not done yet. It is

as though we did not see them stand
like that, so hard trying not
to cheat, to keep the heels flat and

the head level and yet to have grown
another inch. It is as though we
do not know that they don't know

they are not done yet. They are
so big they think so. Yet we know
they are not done and so will go

when we send them, bound in shocks
like brothers, to ripen or to rot
with their mothers' blessings.

Frontier

After the police had taken the man away, after
the papers had been served, after the night
in the safe house was over – the house hidden
in the woods, her truck hidden in another
woman's garage, her friend awake all night

on the couch with her .22 in case – she had
to go back home, alone, to the house where
his face – raging, bloody, drunk – still
boiled outside all the windows, where the door-

frames windowframes seemed still to shake as she
had shaken crouched where she could see but
not be seen, home to the rented house far
from its neighbours, house on a hill, first
house she'd lived in, ever, alone, and loved

coming home to at night, alone, in high piney
dark and stars all down to the valley. After,
when she had to go back home, the hands that
the house had seemed to rest in had become

his hands, the breath that had blown down
from the north over the steep pitched roof
and sung her to sleep nights had become his
liquory breath, had become the voice of the man

who pleads first wheedles and waits and failing,
kicks falls rises cursing, the jaw clenched and the fist
clenched and the crime committed already
in his mind. When she had to, she went

back home and stood alone in her kitchen
with her cat and dog. She knew how many paces
lay between her and the phone, the door,
the yard. She strapped the new .38

onto her hip, turned it till it rested in the small
hollow over her belly, where it seemed to settle
of its own accord, and as she drew water into
the kettle, as she took tea from the canister
and measured it into the pot, she felt the gun's

weight hanging at her waist displace the weight
she had not realized she'd carried – of fear – every
hour to this one of her girl's, her woman's life.

Traditional

She has nothing, neither
power nor wealth, but what
the father of her children
gives her. All is well. She
remains beautiful on a pittance.
They have acquiesced to the stale-
mate that is sex and make do
now with each other's public
desirability, private near-
brushes in the bed each night.
And when war comes and calls for
her sons, though she may sit on
damask or plush and drink red
or white, as she chooses,
and lament to friends, provided
they are women, all, she can but
suffer the loss of what she has
furnished. She cannot toss
her sabots into the gears that
sustain her. She cannot tear the
clothes off her own beautiful
body and barter.

Two Stories for Angel on the
1st Anniversary of Her Sobriety

Minnie Louise, my husband's
great-grandmother, was the one infant
so well hidden when the war party
whooped up over the plains horizon
that she lived through the wagon train massacre.
To thrive. To shake her mane at the sky.

But you are a girl whose mother
was the one who taught her to drink.
Make us a drink, she said on a certain
day, when you got home from school,
before which it had been just,
Angel, Honey, make me a drink.

With you, like that, in the skin
of an afternoon, she could tell herself
for her it was a childhood, and for you
a jump on becoming a big girl: changing
men, changing addresses, pulling
a glow done over you both like
the porch shades down on the landlord.

But we can see her in your eyes,
the woman who bore you: a child who grows
smaller each day that you leave her behind.

No girl is motherless who survives.

Go into your dreams, Angel, to find her
who wrapped you twice – first in lint,
then in her best comforter –
who stoppered your mouth with a sugar teat
and wedged you in the well of the wheel.

Wrought Figure

As though you were rare, you confessed
at our second candle-lit dinner, to your
history: your women. I must confess
each name stung, each one's beauty, gifts
and wit, each one's second language, hair
and eyes, height, even the fights
in which each ended it, or you did.

I'm hard on women, you said. It was
July and night, heavy and fragrant
all around the table set for the
short season out on the porch. Shells
of lobsters, broken, were heaped
on plates, each gruesome body part

a woman scorned. You faced the red
barn, your salt-and-cayenne beard, your
profile inviting the still light my eyes
followed, still wanting you, around and
through the names, the scattered tasty
bits of crustacean. *I love women,*

you said to the barn with a sigh
almost of dread, *especially smart and
pretty ones, Linda*, to the fireflies,
then turned your head to face me, indict
me as victim in the sweet fresh crime.

I took a week, ten days, to think it
through, what you'd said, seeing myself some
time ahead named with the others over
drained shells to some pretty other
woman – and smart – listening. *I'm hard
on men*, I did not confess when you did,
used to not saying so, used to the *used*
in the figure/ground problem of *use*.

Ten days I took to trace the problem
through – figure and ground, ground and
figure, used and user, user and used –
and worked that line back around to its
start, your confession and a circle:
and I love men, pretty and smart, as you are,

*and am not rare in this but, as you
confessed, successful, meaning bested by
fewer than I best.* Let us dance, then, on
the lawn of what's left of summer, and be
not wary as we dance, the smart and the pretty
in the arms of one another, a woman turned by
a man who loves women, and a man turned
by a woman who loves men.

Warrior

Woman after woman forgives you,
child after child, and each horse
is a priest drawn out from the small
door, curtained, that enters

the unscathed chamber. You were
alone there, though, as you told me, as you
told the men who chose you
for what they could make you do

in war. Of course women and children
would be who you turned to
sick again as you are, and horses, the scenes
alive still, page after page of them

in mind. Only you, a loner, could enter
those scenes armed and perform the
unthinkable required. Now you stand
at the heart's door looking in. The boy

they told you was dead sits there, in his Stetson,
a rope in his hand, his eyes on you, quiet,
from across the room. And you are
the grandfather now, who taught you not

to ask why but to do it. You will
not ask him to forgive you. You will
take him, betrayed, to the grave.

The Devil

was a long sleek pelt
of black tom with one fore-
paw across the threshold
of maturity who kept an aging
woman who lived alone
company among the large
animals in the barn.

When she thought them
unobserved, she played
like a girl, dropping onto
her belly — as he did —
to hide behind a blade
of hay, or, miming his tail-
vaulted leap, to spring

from behind and tag him.
When she squatted to piss,
his interest would quicken.
When she swept, having
turned the great ones out
to their day, to a hillside
fan of pastures, he would

ride her shoulder
or lie in a black wedge
of shade. Day, night,
his eyes were the gold
light of an oil lamp. He lay,
when she slept, in her waist's
curve, as a man might.

Blow-Up

Like the telltale grains
in the negative, enlarged and then
enlarged again, printed
and again printed in the movie,

the scene repeats in my mind's
eye, each imprint drawing
the centre nearer, pruning
periphery, unnecessary frame:

luncheon, you across from me
chatting with my beautiful friend,
and dutifully with me. She rises.
Your eyes follow in the look I

know – everyone knows – every-
one knew before you did when it
followed me. Yet as it torques
your head (who hoseys bliss

of self-ignorance in such things)
to watch her rise and go, you
hide it, rubbing your hand
across your face, and,

as though it bothers you,
your near eye, while the other,
covered by its buddy's drama,
soaks up the lithe delicious rising

friend. By the fifteenth time
I've printed it, she's out, and
the room with its hundred other
diners, the table, your red

shirt, the chairs, even the camou-
flaging hand and the eye riding
shotgun. (Men sacrifice depth for
the classic one-eyed glance.)

What gets bigger and bigger,
grotesque in its focus yet somehow
hilarious too, is your brown eye
like a bear in a park shambling
after her, elaborately ogling.
Old and practiced, your iris fills
my silver screen, as she, the beam I
put there, brother, fills yours.

Mercato

for R.G.

At a fountain, you broke open
— for the three of us — figs, the woman
you love, yourself and me the friend

by myself among the circles of shade
made by the yellow umbrellas, by
the gush from the stone lion's mouth.

I put my mouth into the warm flesh,
as you showed me, and sucked the
plush, the delicate grit of seeds

gold and green and roseate as
an Umbria morning. The eyes
you two made at one another,

the smiles wet with nectar, though,
and the handkerchief you gave her
for her hands, her mouth, set me

separate on the stone lip
of the basin. Pigeons resettled
on either side. I turned my face

to dip my hands in the grumble
and gray roar of his water.

Elm Street: October 1977

Up the sidewalk we went together mornings
under the elms, along picket fences
from our temporary, too-expensive
rented quarters: first grade, third grade

children of divorce. I met with their teachers,
pushing my weight of loss before me
like a bus I wasn't licensed to drive:
a pound a day it was taking. Hallowe'en

I walked the charcoal street between them,
so small I wore a costume, too.
Real women opened their doors onto foyers,

music, flowers – homes that petaled
out from them like safe places –
and lavished us with what we could not
buy. Door after door like their father's

I took them away from, the light following
just to the foot of the stairs. A hundred
times that night I took their hands
and drew them with me back into darkness.

Face

On it, eight years sober, age
is catching up to grief
and soon will overpower it:
the net, the delta of
imbricate cells and lines
where the welled tears
spilled under the windows
of the soul – gouged clown-
face of *Captain Haddock* –
have held, have neither
deepened nor crept.

Time and breath
are what have riven the rest,

bent, compressed it.
Where the brow has danced, where
the mouth has answered, where the idea
has skated over the whole surface
in its wild freestyle,
in its sharp skates,
lines of being alive mark now
where the flesh will first
break in the grave: the face
I will not grieve to carry back.

Medicine for the Woman Betrayed

Take this
one gold thing,
which I could not use,
that was a birch wood
on an autumn day,
two horses steaming where they stood
in wands of shallow sunlight,
tea steaming from an open thermos
passed from hand to hand,
bread, apples, a dog, too, who wore
her body as a gladness.
The lie had the fragrance of leafmould. You
were bedding your garden,
path's end and we turned back
before the drop to the lake.
The hour is yours. Unwrap it
from the ignorance in which I kept it
safe enough to carry.
Breath it.

Anniversary

A decade. To the morning. And what
She has forgotten surges up
through her flesh like a current —
that dawn when she woke in the room
beside the children's, alone,
the minutes it took to drag into place
the massive words of the night
before, his absence: his waking
in the bedroom of her friend. As if again`
she were struggling out of that stone
sleep of sedatives he left, her body
is fallen long hours on the live rail
of memory before she remembers:
That was the Gray of a German winter.
That was the winter of dreams
in which he stalked her as a German,
in his helmet of peaked steel,
his gun's muzzle the single glint
in the house that was months of darkness.
Now again it is winter, but here
the snow is light-on-the-ground,
the spruces, in silvery epaulets,
are bearers of light, and the shivering
animal — weak-legged and blind —
that dropped that morning from the body
of innocence has lived to walk among kin.
From deep in these woods of knowing
she turns her head back for the first time,
to reckon the distance overland,
the continental crossing.

Swan Lake: Kenai Wilderness, Alaska
for Diane

July, and the harebells are passing, the red columbine
in her spurs and golden tassles, geraniums of lavender
delicately petalled, frail as insect dimples on the lake.
Dogwood's small blossoms curb the trail like children
sitting, their faces resting on their knees. I think of you
here, so far from gardens, at the lake of your name,
among these brief flowers – not one of which is an *escape*
from the kitchen side of a picket fence. How is your father,
who made, his whole married life, such mockery of
    your mother
elbow-deep in her garden, the world just-that-too-far
from him that he never dared touch her there? *Helpless,*

Daughter of Useless, he called you two as you turned
    the earth
alone together, evening with its carriage of dark climbing
the horizon in the cooling air. *Idleness,* he snorted,
the Devil's Work. Come in. On the trail today lay
scat, grizzly, still warm, red with the undigested flesh
    of salmon.
And in a trampled bed the half-torn bodies. All up the slick
Chickaloon streambed, gouged fish, heads slashed, eggs
unlaid, unfertilized, and monkshood flattened by the
    massive claws.

I was afraid, came back sighting over my shoulder,
laid the heavy bolt across the cabin door. And saw tonight
in my mind's eye the Old Country of such fathers as ours,
framed in the backdoor light, a can in the hand, roaring

out toward their fences, their women. I wish you could
    send him
here to me to study flowers, for by the time he was a man
he'd lost, too, the boy's will to learn. And you, his child,
a grandmother now, still chafing under the boom of his voice,
as you cannot leave your cool green porch and join me,
please grow for us what we did when I lived there,
one green box filled with sturdy geraniums, recusant, red.

Song of the Scullery

Where the plums, where the onions
all day travelled through my hands
the skin is black, like ashes. My hands
look aged, and I am a girl. The master,
who sometimes looks at me as if
he would choose me for a place in his
white bed, now will not look. He visits
to see me beautiful, flowers and pastry
rising, and to write of it on sheets
of white paper. How could I write of it?
The wagons arrive at the door with
the squash, the potatoes. The hunter
knocks with the still-warm bird.
How can you think that of this I might
make a song? Have you never watched them
examine the mare, holding her tongue
out to the side with force in order
with leisure to look within? Ask her
to write of her mouth's interior.
Ask me to write about peeling as I scald,
about scalding as I peel.
I have no song.

Katherine

He was sick, the boy, the second
son – and the daughter, all hope for her
vanished. The man whose names
the heirs would carry, who named them

front to back the way I got to
name the dogs, could care. Later,
I was grateful, fearing what I'd learned
of women only thwarted,

the mother I might have been
to a girl with wings. For sons' flights,
I was born fuel. Now you
arrive, steeled as the girl I was,

the woman, and blue-eyed, blonde
as my firstborn, small as a pot
my body might have thrown,
but cast off by the pair that begot you

in error and regret, and escaped
the pair that took you in
like a side of beef for the steady
family hunger. Poet. Thinker.

Maker. Smiler. Keener, you
are the daughter not of my fertile,
schoolgirl body – machine for making
man's names, man's pride, man's

pleasure – but of my mind, not sexed,
hidden and knowing
in its bloody chamber,
and my heart likewise unhalved:

ugly, therefore, both of them,
and spared
untouchable
– except the one by the other.

"My Fellow Americans . . ."

Arms with hands grasping seek to clutch at the prows.
Bodies thrown recklessly in the way are cut aside.
    W.C. Williams, "The Yachts" 1935

In her office, centre of the many circles
through which one must pass to gain access,
concentric walls of the walled city, over which,

under which, through which I have passed,
one after another these fifty-five years to reach
the Axis Mundi of the American Dream

belatedly, my infant retirement fund a green
spring nubbin on the thick branch of my life,

she asks why I'm using so much costly new
– ten dollars a tablet – migraine medicine, and I
tell her, I admit, I've been giving it to trash,

a young version of myself, a woman twenty-five,
a student, used in her family as a side of beef
hanging in the cool room for its many hungers,

any of its father's appetites, its dirty chores
and weekend window dressing. Twenty years.

She has slashes on her wrists, a slash
around her waist where the father required a fresh
kidney and took it. They are enraged she has

travelled so far from them – hometown girl –
to a frontier place that asks her to write
her life/her life out of it. They stand

in their all-American kitchen and look
at one another with the hungry eyes they had

only for her. When her face pulls away
into its mask of pain, when her eyes become
slits shy of light, her mouth a trembling thread, her

shoulders high and hard as if to carry the freshened
immense weight of her head, which is the
immense weight of her life freshened daily

approaching the next wall of the Dream,
the twenty, thirty to hurdle before she too

perhaps will enter the Temple, the inner sanctum of
health insurance, I share with her my prescription.
And I am betrayer of the invisible hand that

finally gave me the tablet, as my physician's face
tells me, as the pharmacist would. I must not

have suffered enough getting here is the implication,
I must not have been fully taught by my body that

what I was to seek, what I was to find if ever
the last wall crumbled under my touch or yielded
to the axe wielded by my old shoulders

was righteous, isolate and deserving, safe
in my place on the yacht as it drives over.

Letter to the Daughter-in-Heart

The only thing about it that ever hurt them was that I told.
H.L.

I wish I could say they will come around, once
and for all, the family — rapist and his wife,
the other — good — daughter yielding up the new
girlchild to grand-daddy's hand. What I've said
to you already, what I've done out here
before you — not cutting a wide swath but
parting the blades a little to let you pass
forward a little knowing there might be light — has been
in every instance, at every step, for you as well as me,
the least painful, better, way. I've assumed
suicide, always, to be the most painful, if not the
alternative route made clear most heartily by the
family should you veer away from your heart-spot, so
odd a shape, last piece at the centre of the family puzzle.

Today, though, my own heart hurts for you, as it hurts
this long, this late into disclosure, into head-nodding
assent in my own family — *it did happen* — for myself.
It will never go away now, what I told, what I made them
bend their heads to, though they would not say
words, would not give comfort, would never take on even
sorrow for it. I broke off, alone, like a chimney falling
into its stones, and the house still stands, the wound
on the north wall tolerable. There was but the one
place for me, at the juncture of public lie and private
primal power, lines cut into silence before I was born.
Now that my mother has been blessed with forgetting, now

that she can no longer testify, the brother who is family
falls back into the others like a man in an ambulance,
rescued in time, and I'm deprived finally of even the
    right to lie.
It was better, I told you, to know it, to shape it against
the million little lies like tiny upthrust silver olive leaves
in an ancient grove, a single spring olive, same-coloured, tiny,
invisible in stillness or in the wash and sway of wind.
    Something
good would come of it, I said, but now I see they will
    not have me
as I am nor as I was, nor did they ever take me but as slave
and whore that I was born to be, as you were.

Workshop

Another workshop poem of childhood
sexual violation. This week, two
in fact. Sometimes they come in now
thick as fishing poems in spring, thick
sometimes as salmon to the Kenai, as those
old boys on the shore, their rods bobbing,
elbow to elbow, hauling their catches in.

Their ranks are thinning as their hair
thins. Young men in these classes have
something new to look forward to
if they plan to step right up into
Daddy's shoes: the picture that some
words is, a man caught in a flash in a dark
room, his trophy pinned beneath him.

Transit

I cast it away, my body....
Chippewa battle cry

The old man declines in his
time, his own day, which –
sun of his house, sun of his town
that he was, and honoured – he made
as a man in a grader makes road
of his own going.
Think of him then in his going
not as he thinks himself, nor
as his wife does, a child fallen from
your hand – your child to hold
and carry, subdue your own
boldness long and arduously for
 – but as the pathmaker
who, though his road tore into whole wood
crushing brush and sapling,
hidden nests and the visible beds
of those who live by flight,

hauled himself up there
into the seat, the saddle of a life
and kicked it forward. He meant you to remember
this.
He meant to perplex you. Yours
was
the life he rode, yours the childhood
that bore him. Told it was life, moreover,
you let your body be the field

his poisoned body harvested health from.
How – you ask now
your tears starting up as if from a simple
filial love –
take the soul of yourself back
to yourself, incomplete and its stranger,
how rise
in the dark of the other direction
pressing his light down?

Little River
for E.S.

Dear friend, I miss you.
Though you were a flame
in your red jacket, your hair
red-black, it is in green
that I see you – green stones,
barely greater than pebbles, cobbling
the broad river bottom; green water,
shallow, with its cast of brown.
How plumb those fishing days were,
our lines from the two sides of the oxbow
pulled taut to the same angle
in the passing flow. Sitting
back to back like that, I could not
see your eyes. But in the memory
I see them. Of everything, best
I remember them. Brown eyes.
Lights of green.

Spring at the Bunting Institute, 1993

in memoriam, Mary Joe Frug
(feminist legal scholar, murdered 4 April 1992)

> *...the terrorized female body is not that much different*
> *from the sexualized female body.*
> Mary Joe Frug

> *You must live your life as though the revolution had*
> *already taken place.*
> Emma Goldman

> *'Eh, damsel, how like you this for fucking?'*
> from *The Sleeping Beauty*, #12
> Hayden Carruth

I

The last of March, and winter's night-air
gone in a single sunrise. The only dark remaining
is crows, noisy in the treetops, looking heavy as anvils

that shouldn't be up there – couldn't be held up
by what's holding them. Down here in the hive
of our rooms, half circle of buildings for women's work only,

what likewise was unimaginable
and still is singular: women together bending
not to the treadle, to the last machine, but to the mind's

the spirit's labors. All year I have missed you
whom I never knew, who, last minute last year
released from your teaching, was shown to

a room in this building – time, space, quiet,
regard, what women are not born to – as this year I was.

Climbing the steps, I turn back: morning

is a pulse, color rising in a child's cheeks
after fear, after illness, after winter, is the crows,
the red scarf I happen to wear that draws to me red
    from everywhere

is grass hour by hour greening, snowscrim
sootscrim receding, is your absence rising
as the palpable thing, figure out of this spring's ground.

II

God willing, as my mother would say,
in a few months I'll turn fifty. You would have, too:
children near grown, and ahead of you the half-thought
    and unsaid

poised to flourish under your hand
inevitable as bread rising. It could as well be me
a year dead next week, any of us. It could be you still
    writing here

what Law
that undergirds the world beyond our gate
flinches from.

It is whispered there are threats against us.
It is true. Our product is the light
pried out from behind the dark, the coin

hidden under the other coin, the same
and different. We open the heavy ancient
battened doors. We enter

which ought to be enough, after how
many centuries?

III

...historians psychologists theologians artists

novelists poets – geographers, all – we have taken the podium
in those rooms, Culture's Vaticans, have seen
in the eyes of men trapped there by decorum, forced

to listen, rage
lasered on us. I wish
I had been able to listen to you

whom I never heard, only heard of, only read:
thrilled by the terms of your refusal(s): Oldest Heresy
Women's Heresy, to undo the divisions. *Not this*

therefore you are. Every thing, idea, that
to exist must exist split, halved, you dragged back to
      them whole
like the hound wagging into the yard

and tagged with the terms given it by men
-- from the chambers of robes and collar stays backwards
to the streetwords underneath, denied:

noun for the *world*   verb for the *work*
Cunt, you went so far as to say, to say it:
Fuck, what, to the noun, is – first/last – to be done.

IV

You could have gotten grandly by, being silent!
But defying gravity and other laws, delightedly,
your mind riled, as minds are meant to rile,

and riled again by biking by in lipstick,
red hair, in great legs, waving, engaging
the glances of men – in Harvard Square! –

even to policemen, even at your age.

Next week we will plant geraniums.
Shaped like the brain, lipstick red

red hair red geraniums that would speak
their language unafraid, even within earshot
of men. We will set roots in

to remember you. We will read
the very words that you've set, ideas
that now cannot be cut from their life

as you were. Even burned
spine and binding and page, on the street
they would not be subject to the knife

as you were. Oh Sister-Fellow, sister,
woman, thinker, mother – daring
and beautiful – as he opened your legs

as he ribboned your breasts with his blade
taking every root yet to come of you,
did he know?

What can grief learn
in its blindfold of outrage? What
may outrage try to set right

in its hobbles of grief?
But for the blossoms we will set in
to remember you – spirit and flesh together,

that answer – the rest is questions:
his name (who lives still) and from where
in the texts of woman-hating he rose;

the daughter who got to the street
in time to see your life river into the black coat
you'd swooped out in – just for a minute – to see your eyes

lose their crow light; the daughter,
after; the words he   grunted as he did it
his noun   his verb –

(oh husband brother father
stranger son lover)

– to beg, what did you call him?

About the Author

Linda McCarriston is the author of two award-winning collections of poetry, *Talking Soft Dutch* and *Eva-Mary*. The latter was also published by TriQuarterly Books/Northwestern University Press and was a finalist for the National Book Award for Poetry. McCarriston holds both Irish and U.S. citizenship and lives and teaches in Anchorage, Alaska.